Does it bend?
All about stretchy and bendy materials

Anna Claybourne

W
FRANKLIN WATTS
LONDON·SYDNEY

First published in 2009
by Franklin Watts

Copyright © Franklin Watts 2009

Franklin Watts
338 Euston Road
London NW1 3BH

Franklin Watts Australia
Level 17/207 Kent Street
Sydney, NSW 2000

Series editor: Sarah Peutrill
Art director: Jonathan Hair
Design: Elaine Wilkinson
Photographs: Paul Bricknell (unless otherwise credited)

Picture credits: John Alston (6b, 7b), I Stock Photo: 5t (Robert Faric). Pol
Taylor, Bungydome UK Ltd: 24. Rex Features: 24b (Olycom SPA). Science Photo
Library: 21t (Philippe Psaila), 28t (Andrew Brookes, National Physical
Laboratory), 28b (Pascal Goetgheluck), 29 (Volker Steger). Shutterstock: 4b
(Tyler Olson), 5b (Suzanne Tucker), 6t (Ivonne Wierink), 7l (John Lumb), 7r
(Michaela Stejskalova), 9t (Steven Kratochwill), 9b (i9370), 12 and title page
left (Kameel4u), 13b and title page right (Sean Nel), 16 (Vendla Stockdale), 17t
(Paul B. Moore), 17b (Charles Taylor), 20t (Lilac Mountain), 20b (Thien Eu), 21b
(Jan Zoetekouw), 22 (Cathy Keifer), 23t (Daniel Gustavsson), 23bl (Oguz Aral),
25t (Suzanne Tucker). Wishlist images: 10, 11, 23br.
Cover images: Shutterstock: tl (Jan Zoetekouw), tm (Paul B. Moore), tr (Sonya
Etchison), b (Hallgerd).

With thanks to our models: Conah Caple, Mary Conquest, Katie Lloyd, Chris
Penny and Darnell Smith.

Dewey number: 530.4

ISBN 978 0 7496 8720 5

Printed in China

Please note: The investigations in this book have been thoroughly checked and
tested. We regret that the Author and Publisher cannot be held responsible for
any accidents or injury incurred while following the experiments.

Franklin Watts is a division of Hachette Children's Books,
an Hachette UK company.

www.hachette.co.uk

Contents

The topics highlighted above are investigations you can try.

Words in **bold** are in the glossary on page 30.

Stretching and bending

There are stretchy and bendy things all around us. Think of an **elastic** band, a plastic ruler, a stretchy sock or the **spring** in a clothes peg.

Changing shape

There are lots of different kinds of stretchy and bendy **materials**. They all have the same property – they are elastic. You can bend, stretch, squeeze or pull them to make them change shape. When you let go, they spring back to the shape they were to start with.

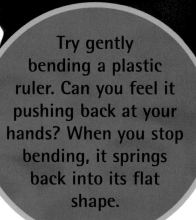

Try gently bending a plastic ruler. Can you feel it pushing back at your hands? When you stop bending, it springs back into its flat shape.

Some materials, such as modelling clay, can be pulled but do not spring back to the same shape. These materials are not elastic.

Pastry can be stretched, but is not elastic. When you roll it out flat, it doesn't spring back into shape.

Useful materials

You can find bendy and stretchy materials in all kinds of everyday objects – from clothes and clickable ballpens to bridges and buildings. Their springy properties are amazingly useful.

A mattress on a bed contains bendy metal springs. When you lie or sit on the mattress, they squash down. The squashed springs push upward, trying to return to their normal shape. This makes the mattress bouncy and comfortable.

A trampoline is made of stretchy material with stretchy springs holding it in place.

Stretchy materials

Some objects are elastic because they are made of stretchy materials. For example, party balloons, elastic bands, **bungee** cords and sewing elastic are all made of materials that stretch.

When you blow up a balloon, the air inside pushes at the **rubber** and makes it stretch more and more.

How stretching works

But why are some materials stretchy, and some not? It's all to do with the pattern of **atoms** in a material – the tiny parts it is made of.

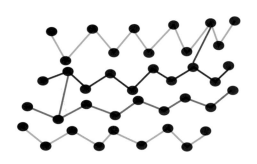

Atoms are joined together in groups called **molecules**. Elastic materials contain long, string-shaped molecules called **polymers**, which are packed together in zigzag shapes. When you pull the material, the molecules stretch out straight. When you let go, they go back to their natural shapes.

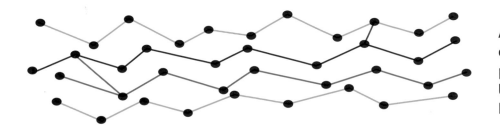

At the top, you can see an elastic polymer molecule packed together. At the bottom, the same molecule has been stretched out.

Sewing elastic keeps clothes such as trousers up!
It stretches when we put the clothes on. As it
tries to spring back into its shorter shape,
it pulls tightly around us.

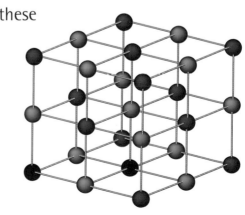

This gymnast is wearing an
elastic fabric leotard that
stretches as she moves.
Have a look at the labels
in your clothes and see
what the stretchiest
clothes are made of.

Not stretchy

Of course, lots of materials aren't very stretchy at all –
like a block of wood, an ice cube or a stone. In these
materials, the atoms are arranged in a fixed grid or block
pattern. The molecules are not like stretchy strings.
Instead, they are shaped more like rigid climbing frames.
If you push, squeeze or pull these
objects, they don't change
shape much at all.

The fixed grid-like structure of
a salt molecule makes a material
that is not elastic.

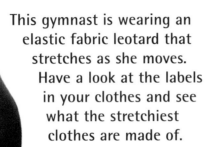

Some objects are not made of very elastic materials, but they are bendy, or **flexible**, because of their shape. They are known as springs.

Special shape

Springs can be made of all kinds of non-elastic materials such as metal, wood or plastic. But to work, they have to be a special shape – such as a flat, thin or spiral shape.

How bending works

Think of a mattress spring made of **steel**. If this steel were a cube, you couldn't stretch it or squash it. But if the steel is made into a spiral-shaped spring, you can squash it and it springs back. How does this happen? When some strong, stiff materials are made into thin or coiled shapes, they can bend and flex a little, as their atoms are pulled away from each other very slightly. But they try to keep their shape, so they spring back when we let go.

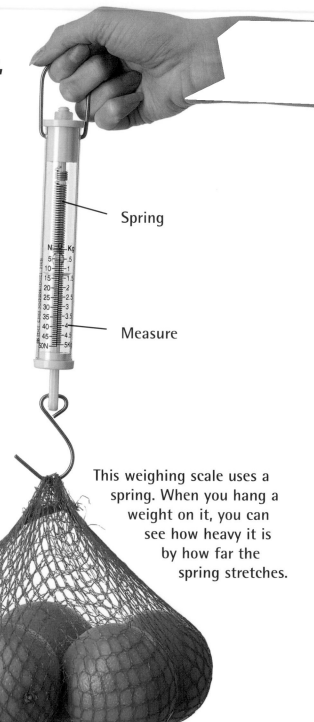

Spring

Measure

This weighing scale uses a spring. When you hang a weight on it, you can see how heavy it is by how far the spring stretches.

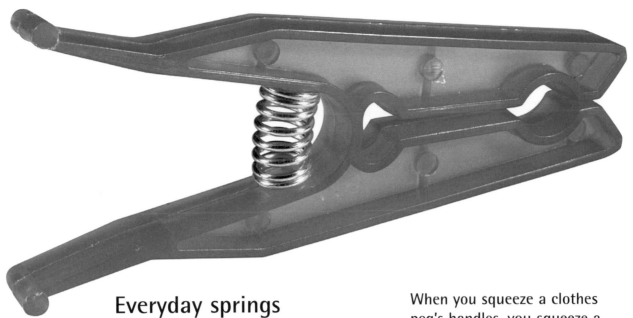

Everyday springs

There are coiled springs in mattresses, clothes pegs, clicking pens and pogo sticks. Try looking closely at a springy clothes peg to see how it works.

When you squeeze a clothes peg's handles, you squeeze a spring in the middle. The spring pushes back, trying to return to its normal shape. This makes the peg grip your washing tightly.

Simple springs

Simpler objects can be springs too. Hairgrips and paperclips, for example, are springy bits of metal. You pull them open to put them on, then they spring back and grip tightly. Metal kitchen tongs work the other way around. You squeeze them to grab something, then when you put them down, they spring apart again.

A paperclip is a very simple spring, made from a bent piece of metal.

Measure the stretch

When you stretch a spring or piece of elastic using weights, it gets longer and longer. But how much longer? Try this experiment to find out.

First, hang, tape or pin the top of the spring or elastic to a table edge, climbing frame or other object so that it can hang down freely.

1

Fix the plastic bag to the lower end of the spring or elastic with sticky tape.

2

Now start adding weights to the bag, one at a time. After adding each one, measure the elastic again.

4

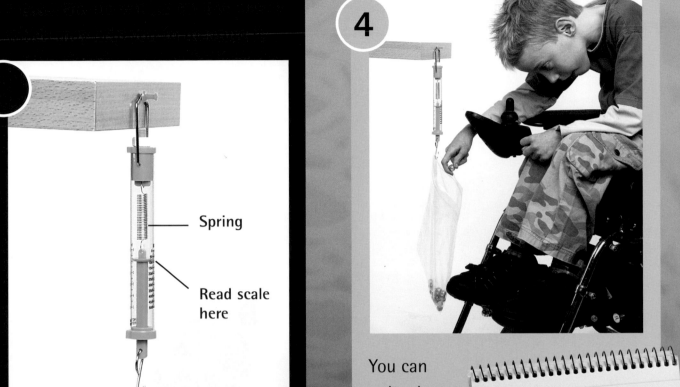

Spring

Read scale here

Plastic bag

You can write down your results like this:

Weight	Length
0 marbles	12cm
1 marble	...
2 marbles	...
3 marbles	...
4 marbles	...

Make a graph

You can plot your results as dots on a graph too, then use a line to join them. What do you notice?

When the stretching stops

As you've probably noticed, nothing can stretch or bend forever. You can't stretch an elastic band around the world!

If there's too much bending or pulling force, the spring or elastic stops working. It reaches a point called the **elastic limit**. After that, it isn't elastic any more.

What happens?

Different types of elastic materials and springs behave in different ways. If you stretch sewing elastic too far, it will just stop stretching. Some materials, such as an elastic band, could snap if you pull them too far.

You know that when you blow bubble-gum up (top), you have to be careful not to fill it up with too much air. If it gets too big, and the gum can't stretch any more ... POP! (left).

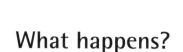

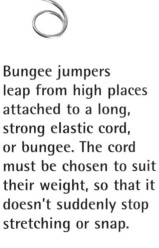

Stretched springs

If you stretch a spring too far, it may suddenly lose its springy shape completely. After this, it will no longer spring back to the shape it was to start with.

The spring on the left has been stretched beyond its elastic limit. It can no longer return to the shape it was to start with (shown on the right).

Bungee jumpers leap from high places attached to a long, strong elastic cord, or bungee. The cord must be chosen to suit their weight, so that it doesn't suddenly stop stretching or snap.

No going back

A paperclip is a type of spring. When you use it, you pull it apart slightly. It tries to spring back, holding your paper in place. But how far will it bend?

You will need:

A large stack of A4 paper (it can be used again), a notepad and pen and a selection of unused paperclips of different sizes and materials, such as metal, coated metal and plastic (make sure no one minds if they can't be used again, as some may get broken).

Choose one type of paperclip, and use it to clip five sheets of paper together.

Then take the paperclip off carefully, and check it hasn't changed shape. It should still lie flat on the table.

Now try the same test with other types and sizes of paperclip. Which can hold the most paper before changing shape? Do any of the clips actually break?

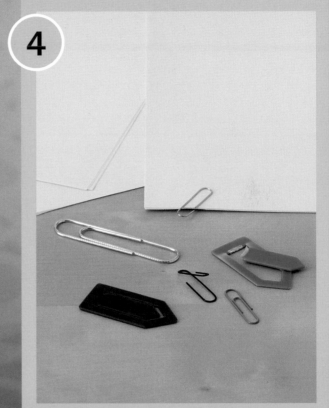

You can write down your results like this:

Clip	Elastic limit	What happened?
Small metal paperclip	20 sheets	Bent
Large metal paperclip	55 sheets	...
Plastic-coated paperclip	...	...
Large plastic paperclip	...	...

Energy store

Springs and elastic materials hold a store of **energy**. Energy is the power to do work or make things happen.

For example, when you squeeze a spring, you use energy. The energy is stored in the spring, waiting to be released. When you let go, the energy is released as the spring boings back into shape.

Useful energy

This has all kinds of handy uses. A diving board, for example, is a big, flat spring. When you jump on the end, you use energy to bend the spring and push it down. Then the stored energy is released as the board springs back, pushing you up.

Boinggg! A springy diving board helps a diver bounce into the air.

Bows and arrows work the same way. A bow is a strong spring. When the string is pulled back, the bow bends and stores energy. When the archer lets go, the bow springs back, pulling on the string and firing the arrow.

An archer uses lots of energy to bend a bow, storing up energy to fire the arrow.

Winding up

Clockwork toys and wind-up clocks use a spring to hold a store of energy. Then they release it slowly, to provide power. The unwinding spring gradually pushes around the clock's hands or the toy's wheels or other moving parts.

When you wind up a clockwork toy, you make the spring inside coil up tightly. As the spring unwinds to get back to its original shape, it makes the toy move.

Elastic-powered fan

You will need:

At least three plastic straws, ideally strong, non-bendy ones, a large elastic band (about 10cm long), a metal paperclip, scissors and a piece of stiff card.

This easy-to-make machine uses an elastic band to hold a store of energy. As you twist the band, it stretches and stores up energy ready to be released. When you let go, the energy makes the elastic band untwist, and the fan spins round.

Cut a piece of straw the same length as the elastic band, and another piece about 3cm long.

1

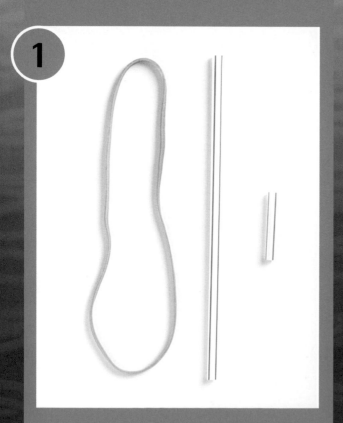

2

Hook the paperclip into one end of the elastic band, and feed the other end of the elastic band through the piece of straw (you may need to use a pipe cleaner or narrow stick to push it through).

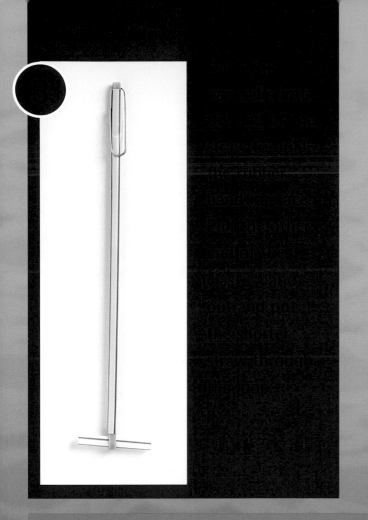

Cut out two rectangles of card, each 2cm by 4cm, to make the fan blades. Cut two slits in each end of the short straw, and fit the blades into them to make a fan shape. The slits should be in different positions, as in the picture, so that the two fan blades do not line up.

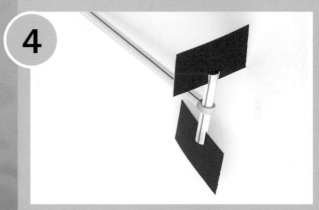

Now, holding the longer straw, wind the fan part round and round with your finger – wind it up quite a lot. Let go, and the fan should spin round fast enough to make a light breeze.

What would happen?

What happens if you twist the fan one way and then the opposite way? Can you see how a similar device could be used to make an elastic-powered aeroplane?

Making elastic and springs

Right now, factories all over the world are busy making stretchy elastic fabrics, elastic bands and millions of springs of all shapes and sizes for many different uses.

Aircraft like this glider need very big, strong springs in their landing gear, so that they bounce a little when they land.

Making elastic bands

Elastic bands are made from rubber, a naturally elastic material that comes from a type of tree. A machine heats the rubber and forces it through a ring-shaped hole, so that it comes out as a tube. Then the tube is sliced up into sections to make the elastic bands.

The white liquid in the pot is latex, or rubber tree sap. It is being collected from the tree to make rubber.

Stretchy fabrics

Stretchy fabrics for clothes are usually made by mixing normal fabric, such as cotton or nylon, with strands of stretchy material. It could be rubber, or a human-made elastic polymer, such as spandex.

This loom at a fabric factory weaves strands of stretchy spandex together with other fibres such as cotton, to make soft, elastic fabrics.

Making springs

A spring starts off as a piece of wire, made by heating metal and pulling it out to form a long string. A set of rollers push the wire through a machine so that it coils around a metal cylinder called a **mandrel**, forming a spiral shape.

Stretchy structures

Tall buildings need to bend a little, to sway in the wind. Suspension bridge **cables** stretch slightly when a heavy load is on the bridge, then spring back. These things must be made of materials that are elastic enough, but not so elastic that the structures wobble or fall over!

A suspension bridge uses slightly stretchy metal cables to hold up the road or walkway.

Elastic and springs in nature

As well as springs and elastic from factories, we're surrounded by elastic in the natural world. Even our own bodies have elastic parts.

Stretchy spider silk

Spider silk is one of nature's stretchiest substances. Being stretchy helps to make a spider's web stronger, as it can be blown by the wind, or pulled down by heavy raindrops, without breaking.

Amazing tongue

A chameleon's tongue is incredibly stretchy too. The chameleon shoots it out of its mouth to catch insects. The tongue can stretch up to six times its normal length!

This chameleon has used its stretchy, sticky tongue to catch some lunch.

Bendy trees

Tree branches are natural springs. They bend in the wind, then spring back, instead of breaking off. Palm trees, which often grow on coasts, have the bendiest of all tree trunks. They can survive **hurricane** winds without snapping.

Bendy palm trees often stay standing in hurricanes, even when buildings collapse.

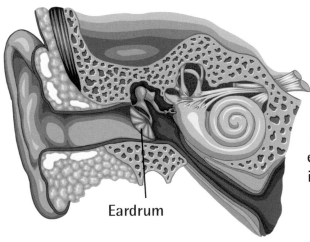

Eardrum

This diagram shows where your eardrum is, deep inside your ear.

Our elastic bodies

Some parts of our bodies have to be elastic to work properly. Our **eardrums** are stretchy **membranes**, or thin sheets, inside our ears. We hear when sounds make our eardrums stretch slightly, and wobble or **vibrate** to and fro.

We also have stretchy parts called **vocal cords** in our throats. The more tightly we stretch them, the higher the noise we make when we speak or sing.

How high and low can you sing? To make a higher sound, you are stretching your vocal cords and making them tighter. Rest your hand on your throat to see if you can feel the stretch.

Elastic and springs in sports and games

Everyone seems to love bouncing and boinging around. We use stretchy and springy materials and equipment for lots of sports, games and fun activities.

Bouncy balls

A bouncy ball, whether it's solid rubber or full of air, uses elastic properties. When it hits the ground, it squashes into a flatter shape, storing energy. Then it springs back and bounces up again. Football, tennis, basketball and dozens of other sports depend on balls being bouncy.

Trampolines

When you jump on a trampoline, you stretch it out of shape. Then it boings back, pushing you up high.

In this Bungydome – you bounce super-high on a trampoline while attached to strong, stretchy bungee cords.

Jumping even higher

Diving boards and gym springboards also use the way some materials store energy to help us jump much higher than we can normally. In pole vaulting, athletes can jump over six metres (more than three times average adult height) using energy stored by bending a long pole, then springing up on it.

A pole vaulter springs into the air. Vaulting poles are made from **fibreglass** or **carbon fibre**.

Flexi feet

We can now even wear special artificial springy feet, made from carbon fibre. Sometimes dancers attach them to their shoes to allow them to leap high into the air. People who have lost their legs or feet can also wear these amazing springy feet for running and jumping

Artificial feet like these are made of springs. When the runner lands, the spring bends and stores energy, then pushes him up again.

Ruler diving board

Recreate the **springy** effect of a diving board using a ruler and toy 'divers'. When you push the ruler down, you store energy, ready to push the diver up into the air.

Position the ruler so that two thirds of it is sticking out over the edge of the table, and hold it in place with a pile of books.

Place the washing-up bowl on the floor under the end of the ruler, and half-fill with water.

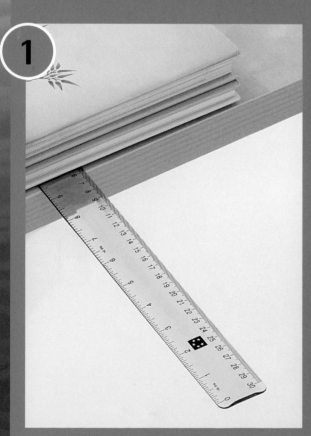

1

2

Experiment with getting the toy figures to dive into the 'pool'. Does the diving board work better if you press more gently or harder? Can you get the figures to do a somersault?

4

TAKE CARE:
Make sure an adult helps you with any experiment, and don't get your eyes too near the ruler.

What would happen?

What happens if you make the diving board longer or shorter? Is there a point where it stops working as well?

New inventions and the future

Inventors are still coming up with new types of elastic, and new uses for stretchy and bendy materials.

Bendy electronics

Electric **circuits** are usually found in computers and other gadgets, mounted on a stiff board. But inventors have now found a way to make a whole electronic circuit out of bendy, elastic materials. These bendy circuits can be sewn into clothes, for example to make a safety jacket with flashing lights on it. One day, they could even be built into our bodies.

Stretchy, bendy circuits can form all kinds of shapes.

Memory metals

Memory metal is made using two metals called nickel and titanium. An object, such as a pair of glasses, made from memory metal can be completely twisted and squashed out of shape, then spring right back to normal. This is great for making unbreakable spectacles.

These memory metal glasses aren't broken – they'll spring back into perfect shape.

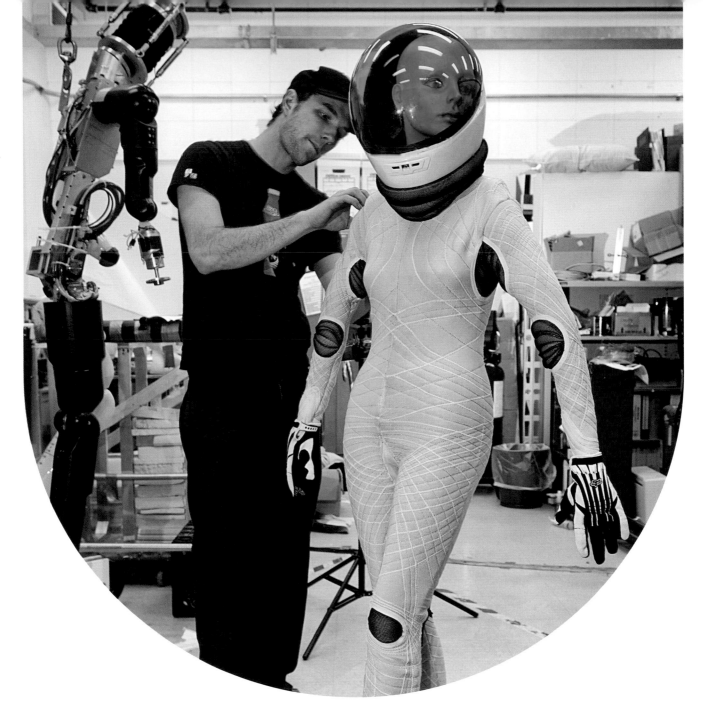

Stretchy space suits

Astronauts need suits that press in on their bodies, to make up for the lack of **air pressure** in space. Traditional space suits are filled with air to create pressure, but this makes them very bulky. Now, new space suits are being designed using very strong elastic fabric that squeezes the body all over. These suits will make it much easier to move around in space.

A dummy wearing an early version of an elastic space suit.

Glossary

air pressure The pressure, or pressing force, of the air that is around us all the time on Earth.

atoms The tiny units that materials are made up of.

bungee A very strong, thick elastic cord.

cables Strong ropes made of metal.

carbon fibre A very light, strong material made using tiny strands of a substance called carbon.

circuit A loop made up of wires and other parts that electricity can flow around.

eardrum A tightly stretched skin inside the ear that detects sound in the air.

elastic Able to stretch, then return to its original shape.

elastic limit The point at which an elastic material is stretched so far that it loses its elasticity.

energy The power to do work or make things happen.

fibreglass A substance made up of very thin glass strands.

flexible Another word for bendy.

hurricane A powerful wind storm that forms over the sea.

loom A machine used to weave fabrics.

mandrel An object used to shape other objects.

materials The different types of stuff, or matter, that things are made from.

membrane A thin, stretchy sheet of skin-like material.

molecules Tiny building blocks that materials are made of, made up of atoms.

polymer A molecule shaped like a long string or chain.

rubber A natural elastic material made from the sap of the rubber tree.

spring An elastic object that can be stretched or squashed, but then returns to its original shape.

steel A kind of very strong metal, made from iron mixed with carbon and other substances.

vibrate To shake quickly back and forth.

vocal cords Elastic parts inside our throats that stretch to change the pitch of our voices.

Some answers

Page 11: You should find a straight line appears on the graph. Strings and elastic stretch the same amount whenever you add the same amount of force. A scientist named Robert Hooke discovered this in 1676, and it is known as Hooke's Law.

Pages 14-15: You may find that metal paperclips lose their elasticity and change shape, while plastic paperclips are more likely to break. This is because plastics are often more brittle than metals, and not as strong.

Page 19: If you twist the fan one way, it blows air towards you. If you twist it the other way, it pushes air backwards.

Page 23: Men and boys can usually sing the lowest notes, while women and girls can sing the highest notes. Men's vocal cords are longer and thicker, and harder to stretch tight.

Page 27: If the ruler is too short, it will not be bendy enough, and it may be hard to make the diver spring off. If it's too long, it may become wobbly and hard to control. Try to find the best length for making the highest dives.

Index

Further information

Books to read

Materials by Carol Ballard (Wayland, 2008)

Investigating Science: Using Coins, Paper and Rubber Bands by Jan Kaslow (Silverleaf Press, 2008)

Amazing Rubber Band Cars: Easy-to-Build Wind-Up Racers, Models, and Toys by Mike Rigsby (Chicago Review Press, 2007)

Balloon Science Action Pack by Chris Oxlade (Top That Publishing, 2000)

Flexible and Rigid by Angela Royston (Heinemann, 2008)

Material World: Rubber by Claire Llewellyn (Franklin Watts, 2005)